IMAGES OF W

CARNAGE:
THE GERMAN FRONT
IN WORLD WAR ONE

RARE PHOTOGRAPHS FROM WARTIME ARCHIVES

Alistair Smith

Pen & Sword
MILITARY

First published in Great Britain in 2012 by
PEN & SWORD MILITARY
an imprint of
Pen & Sword Books Ltd,
47 Church Street,
Barnsley,
South Yorkshire.
S70 2AS

Copyright © Alistair Smith 2012

A CIP record for this book is available from the British Library.

ISBN 978 1 84884 682 1

The right of Alistair Smith to be identified as Author of this work
has been asserted by him in accordance with the Copyright,
Designs and Patents Act 1988.

All rights reserved. No part of this book may be reproduced or
transmitted in any form or by any means, electronic or mechanical
including photocopying, recording or by any information storage and
retrieval system, without permission from the Publisher in writing.

Typeset by Concept, Huddersfield, West Yorkshire
Printed and bound in England by CPI Group (UK) Ltd, Croydon, CR0 4YY.

Pen & Sword Books Ltd incorporates the Imprints of Pen & Sword Aviation,
Pen & Sword Family History, Pen & Sword Maritime, Pen & Sword Military,
Pen & Sword Discovery, Wharncliffe Local History, Wharncliffe True Crime,
Wharncliffe Transport, Pen & Sword Select, Pen & Sword Military Classics, Leo Cooper,
The Praetorian Press, Remember When, Seaforth Publishing and Frontline Publishing

For a complete list of Pen & Sword titles please contact
Pen & Sword Books Limited
47 Church Street, Barnsley, South Yorkshire, S70 2AS, England
E-mail: enquiries@pen-and-sword.co.uk
Website: www.pen-and-sword.co.uk

Contents

Introduction **4**

Chapter One
Before the Battle **9**

Chapter Two
Preparing for Battle **27**

Chapter Three
The Trenches **35**

Chapter Four
The Enemy **62**

Chapter Five
The Aircraft **72**

Chapter Six
War Damages **88**

Chapter Seven
Official Photographs **106**

Bibliography **125**

Dedication

The author would like to dedicate this book
to the memory of Peter Coles

Introduction

On 1 January 2008, arguably the last German infantryman of the First World War, Erich Kaestner, died in Hanover at the age of 107 years. Admittedly Kaestner had only been called up in July 1918, but he did take part in one of the last German pushes to turn the tide.

Approximately 2 million German soldiers were killed during the course of the First World War and a further 4.2 million were wounded. In addition to this, 1 million soldiers of the Austro-Hungarian Empire were also killed and 3.6 million were wounded.

This album belonged to an unnamed German infantry soldier. It is clear from the photographs that he saw action in the trenches on the Western Front. He was also able to take photographs of downed enemy aircraft and enemy prisoners of war, which supposes that at some stage he was responsible for guarding them.

The spark that set off the First World War took place hundreds of miles away from the killing fields of France and Belgium. The heir to the Habsburg throne, Archduke Franz Ferdinand, was visiting Sarajevo in Bosnia. The whole region had been annexed by the Austro-Hungarians in 1908. The Serbs living in Bosnia were highly resentful that the country had not been incorporated into Serbia itself. A student, Gavrilo Princip, assassinated both Franz Ferdinand and his wife. This incident took place on 28 June 1914. A month later the Austro-Hungarian Empire declared war on Serbia.

The Russians then sided with the Serbs and began their mobilisation. On 1 August Germany declared war on Russia, and France began to mobilise. Two days later Germany declared war on France and on 4 August they invaded Belgium. Great Britain sent Germany an ultimatum demanding her withdrawal, but there was no reply and, consequently, Britain declared war on Germany.

The First World War was by no means the first conflict to be extensively photographed. In fact photographs had been taken during the Crimea War, the Indian Mutiny, the American Civil War, the Spanish-American War and the Second Boer War. Nonetheless, for the professional photographer, chronicling the conflict was extremely difficult. The British, for example, arrested several reporters and photographers in France in 1915. Civilian photographers were generally banned and in fact the penalty for taking photographs at the front was death. However, there are tens of thousands of photographs of the First World War, many of which were taken by photographic agencies or by officers with the necessary finance, equipment and skill to take their own private shots. Unfortunately many of the photographs that were

Archduke Franz Ferdinand, who was assassinated along with his wife in Sarajevo, Bosnia, a recently annexed Austrian province. *(Library of Congress)*

taken during the First World War are uncredited. If anything the photographs are simply attributed to official photographers. There is very little existing documentation to help us identify the names of photographers, some of which took extreme risks in the trenches.

The First World War was a calamitous conflict, not just for the Allies, but also for Germany and its allies. This photographic album vividly portrays the squalor of trench warfare. We can see from the photographs the realities of living in the mud and cold. We can also see the devastation caused by constant bombardment, the way in which the landscape had been churned by thousands of shells many of which buried hundreds if not thousands of men.

Although many of the locations of these photographs may never be known, this photographic album provides a vivid testimony of the First World War from the rare German perspective.

An entire generation of young men were killed, maimed or permanently traumatized by their involvement in the First World War. Statistics cannot even begin to explain the experience. Not only did the First World War leave a lasting legacy on families across the world, but it also served as a catalyst in the rise of Hitler and a convenient excuse for him to redress the wrongs that he perceived had been inflicted on Germany by the Treaty of Versailles.

As far as the British are concerned, the Commonwealth War Graves Commission maintains 385 cemeteries in Belgium alone. There is a staggering 1,665 in France. These cemeteries are for those who fell from Britain and her Empire.

Nothing could have prepared the world for the kind of conflict that would develop, particularly in Europe, on the Western Front. The Germans knew that they would have to ultimately fight on two fronts, probably against France and Russia. A plan that had been developed between 1897 and 1905, known as the Schlieffen, counted on Russia taking at least six weeks to mobilise. The plan called for a huge, sweeping movement across Belgium and Luxembourg, which would hook around Paris and roll up the French army from the north. Changes were made to the plan before the Germans launched their assault, attacking in five columns on 5 August 1914. Enemy defences and troops proved to be more resilient, but the Germans had still made considerable progress.

By late August the British Expeditionary Force had been thrown into the line at Mons, where they fought their first land battle in Western Europe since Waterloo in 1815. The Germans, however, still held the upper hand and continued to push west and south, capturing swathes of Belgium and France in the process. On the River Marne, Allied counterattacks saved Paris and condemned that sector of the front to trench warfare. Elsewhere on the front there was still movement, but as Allied lines began to stiffen, and even advance, these areas also were reduced to stalemate.

Here we see Field Marshal Paul von Hindenburg, Kaiser Wilhelm II and General Ludendorff. Until becoming Chief of the General Staff in August 1916 Hindenburg was Commander-in-Chief of German forces in the east. Ludendorff exercised enormous power over the military and the German economy. As a right-winger he also took part in the Munich Putsch of 1923. Wilhelm II became Emperor of Germany in 1888 but was forced to abdicate after Germany's defeat in 1918. *(Library of Congress)*

Battles such as Ypres, Verdun, Arras, Cambrai and Amiens are etched into the memory of those who may only have a scant knowledge of the First World War.

It would take until 1918 before the tide finally turned once and for all against Germany. Almost precisely four years since the outbreak of the war the Allies were striking back. On 8 August 1918, for example, during the battle of Amiens, the British III Corps inflicted 27,000 casualties, including 15,000 prisoners, on the Germans and destroyed 400 of their guns.

By late September 1918, with the German Hindenburg Line breached, Germany and her allies began to put out feelers seeking peace. As each day passed the German army continued to be pummelled and pushed back. Their powers of resistance were diminishing and the Allies were in no mood to allow Germany a cheap peace. All, however, was not well in the Allied camp: the British Expeditionary Force had been depleted in number and was exhausted. The American army was not fully combat ready and the British distrusted the abilities of the French. Yet more breakthroughs were achieved. On 1 November the US Army broke through to cut the Lille to Metz railway, the Canadian Corps had made strong progress, as had the New Zealand Division.

Turkey had signed an armistice at the end of the October and, at the same time, the German High Seas Fleet mutinied. The end was coming. The Kaiser abdicated, the German Republic was created and at 0500 hours on 11 November 1918 the armistice was finally signed. It fell to the Canadians to clear Mons of the Germans at dawn and at 1100 hours on the 11th day of the 11th month peace finally reigned across Europe.

*   *   *

This photographic album is owned by the collector James Payne. The authors are indebted to him and would direct any reader that wishes to obtain their own copies of the photographs to visit the website (www.throughtheireyes2.co.uk) which is his own military photo archive.

Chapter One

Before the Battle

The German states had only been united in 1871, but its military traditions had existed for more than a hundred years. Many of the smaller states had been absorbed by the Prussian system, with numbered regiments for example, but many still retained vestiges of their older identities with badges and titles.

The German army had a number of regular line regiments; supported by reserve regiments (each numbered and made up of demobilised soldiers). Backing these up were the *Landwehr* regiments and the *Landsturm*. Most of the regular army was made up of conscripts. Men would be expected to serve two years as infantry (or three if in the artillery or cavalry). After this initial period of service, the men would then be reservists for the next four or five years. Reservists were expected to make themselves available for training periods which were put on twice a year. After this period of service, the men would find themselves in the *Landwehr*. Their service would last another eleven years (or until they were thirty-nine). At this point, the men were finally transferred into the *Landsturm* (usually until the age of forty-five).

Although the majority of German soldiers could expect to be conscripted at the age of twenty, nominally all German males over the age of seventeen were on the *Landsturm* lists (this practice dated back to the Napoleonic times).

The pre-war German army stood at around 800,000 men, however by Christmas 1914, this had rapidly expanded to a staggering 5 million. By 1917, the German army stood at a strength of approximately 7 million. The key to this was the fact that the Germans could draw on a reserve (in 1914) of some 4.3 million trained soldiers. They were organised on some twenty Army Corps which collectively boasted eighty-seven infantry divisions and eleven cavalry divisions.

When the mobilisation orders were made in 1914, the *Landwehr* and *Landsturm* were immediately available for defence. Many were brought straight into new reserve divisions and corps which could be deployed as front-line troops.

As we will see in this collection of photographs, the German soldier had an impressive array of uniforms ranging from the ceremonial to the practical combat clothing. Equally, we can see some of the variations in uniform, as elements of regional differences remain in some of the detailing of the uniforms.

What is noticeable in these photographs is the absence of the *Pickelhaube* (spiked helmet). The dress version of polished black leather was replaced with the more practical pressed leather or felt model, either in rush green or field grey. This peculiar form of headgear had been introduced to Prussian infantry regiments in 1842. It had gone through several variations and developments, such as improvements to the chinstrap and the size of the spike, as well as the adoption of cloth covers.

The dress uniform of German troops was a dark blue jacket. The trousers would also tend to be dark blue, usually tucked inside long, marching boots. In the majority of cases the soldiers would wear a *Mutz* in a variety of different designs, some with peaks and some without. The *Pickelhaube* was eventually dispensed with and replaced with a Model 1916 steel helmet. This was largely as a result of a disproportionate number of head wounds due to the lack of protection provided by the *Pickelhaube*. The original German helmets were extremely heavy and after some tests it was decided that a universal issue of metal helmets would be made. They were supposed not to exceed 1kg in weight and they also needed to ensure that they provided good all-round vision, so this placed a practical limit on the side and neck skirt.

(*Opposite page*) Back in the spring of 1910 it was decided that regiments would be equipped with a field grey uniform. Officially coloured dress uniforms were abandoned in 1915 when a new field grey dress uniform was introduced. This is a typical loose fitting jacket with eight nickel or zinc copper alloy buttons. Unit markings would specify particular regiments. Infantry and machine gunners would have scarlet piping, jager had green piping, artillery and pioneers had red piping to the body of the jacket and a black collar and medical staff would have dark blue piping. This individual is an officer, who would have had to pay for his own uniform. This is a portrait of the owner of the original album and seems to suggest that he is the recipient of the Military Merit Medal, this was in silver. It was issued between 1892 and 1918. It had the head of King Wilhelm II of Württemberg on the face (looking to the right) on the reverse it read '*FÜR TAPFERKEIT UND TREUE*' (For bravery and loyalty). This motto was written inside a wreath of laurel. The medal was originally introduced in 1818 for military merit. This new version was introduced when Wilhelm II became king on 6 October 1891 (the medal itself was brought in on 26 June 1892).

A posed studio shot can be seen here. This individual is probably a reservist and is simply holding the cavalry sabre as a prop for the photograph. He is wearing a peak-less *Mutz*, which is an 'other ranks' cap and would probably have had scarlet piping. The jacket would normally have been field grey, although in this instance he appears to be wearing his dress uniform, which was a single breasted, dark blue jacket, with matching trousers. It is not possible to see any unit insignia in this photograph.

German soldiers are posing on the bridge in this photograph. Note the two styles of *Mutzen*. Both men have peaked caps; the peaked version was known as the *Dienstmutze*, or service cap. The visorless version, the *Feldmutz* (field cap) were mainly either field grey or grey-green, so that they would match the rest of the uniform. In the trenches it would be the *Feldmutz* that was most frequently worn, along with the fatigue uniform. The service cap had a black, leather peak with a chinstrap and it tended to be worn by officers or non-commissioned officers in the trenches, but by all ranks in rear areas. Essentially it was for formal situations or as part of the walking out uniform. They were differentiated by the arm of the service and the state to which the troops belonged. For example, infantry would have a scarlet cap band and piping, whereas an artilleryman would have a black cap band and scarlet edging with scarlet piping. The field cap was usually worn with a coloured cap band but this would be covered in grey cloth.

Three German soldiers in a cabin in a camp are shown in this photograph. The two men to the left and right of the photograph are probably officers, although it is difficult to pick out their insignia on the shoulder straps. The simplicity of their uniforms suggests that these men could well be reservists and are wearing standard field grey uniforms with scarlet piping and Swedish style cuffs. Within a week of the outbreak of the war the reservists had been called up. The standard uniform was the M1907/10 tunic, and the M1895 belt was made of tan leather. The belt buckle plates varied according to where the regiments had originally been based.

This is a fascinating photograph showing the range of different uniform variations in the German army. In 1910, German officers had the choice of seven uniforms. These included the *Gesellschaftsanzug* (formal ceremonial uniform), the *Galaanzug* (parade uniform), *Strassenanzug* (walking out uniform), *Dienstanzug* (service uniform), *Kleiner Dienstanzug* (undress uniform) and the *Feldmarachmasser Anzug* (field uniform). The latter uniform was field grey and brought into service in 1910. From 1914, the service, undress and walking out uniforms were all adapted to make use of field grey material. Non-commissioned officers and other ranks had a bewildering nine uniforms. They had a parade uniform, walking out, undress, guard, service, reporting and fatigue dress. In addition to this, there was also, from 1907, the field and training uniforms. The first seven uniforms could trace their design all the way back to 1842. The man fourth from the left seated, may be wearing the Kaiser Wilhelm I Centenary Medal. This was a circular gilt bronze medal. It had on its face a head and shoulders portrait of Kaiser Wilhelm I in full military uniform facing right. It was inscribed '*WILHELM DER GROSSE DEUTSCHER KAISER*' (Wilhelm the Great German Emperor) and '*KOENING VON PREUSSEN*' (King of Prussia). On the reverse '*ZUM ANDENKEN AN DER HUNDERSTEN GEBURTSTAG DES GROSSEN KAISERS WILHELM I 1797 – 22 MAERZ – 1897*' was inscribed (roughly translated as 'in commemoration of the hundredth birthday of the great Kaiser Wilhelm I 1797 – 22 March – 1897'). There was also a cushion bearing the *Hohenzollern* or Prussian crown and orb on a sword, with a laurel branch on the left and an oak branch on the right. The medal was awarded on 22 March 1897 to all veterans of the wars of 1864, 1866 and 1871. The medal was struck using Austrian, Danish and French cannon metal. It was designed by Walter Schott.

This is an early 360 degree photograph of our German soldier, taken from each conceivable angle and developed as a single image by the photographer. It is clear that the photographer has stitched the shots together to create a fascinating image of the subject. It is still not possible to identify his regiment or rank. The image is still reversed in places, due to the process used by the photographer, but it is just possible to make out the numbers 22 on the shoulder of the man. This may suggest that he was part of *Infanterie-Regiment Keith (1. Ober-schlesisches) Nr.22* or *Reserve-Infanterie-Regiment Keith (1. Ober-schlesisches) Nr.22*. If the latter, then it was part of the 12th Reserve Division mobilised in August 1914 and the majority of the men were recruited from mainly Upper Silesia.

A relaxed, posed shot showing the owner of the original album in the centre. We can clearly see the three button arrangement on his cuffs. He is wearing the most common variant, known as the Brandenburg. The cuff patterns on the *Waffenrock* (field service uniform) were mainly the Brandenburg, Swedish, Saxon or French. The Brandenburg had an oblong flap with three buttons. The Saxon had two buttons separated by piping, the Swedish had two buttons arranged below the piping and the French had three vertical buttons. He also wears a *Dienstmutz* with a black leather peak and chinstrap. This would have been worn by all ranks behind the lines. It was an integral part of the walking out dress (and for more formal occasions). It was well-shaped with a stiffened crown.

Some magnificent facial hair on display here as a group of German soldiers pose in their walking out uniforms, this shot was probably taken inside a training or transit camp just before the outbreak of the war. After 1915, it became clear that the German army needed a far more practical uniform. The new field service dress was announced in September. The new uniform was essentially a blouse in loose fitting field grey (other units had grey-green such as *Jager*). The blouse had a simpler collar and cuffs, the buttons were duller and there was no piping on the body of the jacket. The new uniform never really completely replaced the older uniforms, in fact as late as 1918 it was common to see a mix of uniforms. By that stage, newer uniforms were somewhat shabby as they had to be made using cheaper fabrics or recycled materials.

This is a group of *Landsturm* posing on a German street with friends and families. They are wearing a basic oilskin cap with a metal *Landwehr* Cross (above the *Landes* or State cockade). They do not have any collar insignia visible; normally they would be wearing an armband with the location where the battalion was raised. Even the crosses were not standardized as such, the Prussian cross was the norm, but the Bavarian, Saxon and Hesse cities, for example were all different and had different mottos. As might be expected in times of war, there were not enough oilskin caps to issue to all units, instead, some units were issued old *Landwehr* shakos. Many units were still holding these in store, and simply reissued them.

Königslager

A group of German soldiers in a military camp. For Germans, there were two different types of military manpower; those eligible for active military service (the *Dienstplicht* and the *Landwehr*) and then the *Landsturm*. The whole system was designed to cover the ages seventeen to forty-five. This was a reflection of the traditional German military service model dating back to the Napoleonic wars where there would be a professional army (the first two categories) and a People's Army (essentially the *Landsturm*). The active military service component (the *Dienstplicht*) covered the regular forces as well as the reserve forces. Not all of the men were conscripted as there was also a class of volunteers (*Freiwilliger*). These were broken down into two groups – the enlisted volunteers serving for two to four years. The other group were those that volunteered for a single year of service. Despite this, the vast majority of German soldiers were drafted, and only around 6 per cent of the available manpower had actually volunteered.

A faded, but fascinating shot of German soldiers relaxing in a training camp is seen here. In 1914 most of the enlisted men would be wearing a coarse, field grey, wool fatigue tunic. It was loosely cut, which would allow them to wear another field tunic underneath it to keep them warm. Their shoulder straps, which were also field grey, would have a company number, and these were often rolled up in order to hide the unit number. The buttons, made from galvanized iron, were introduced at the beginning of 1915. A simplified version of the field uniform was manufactured from March to July 1915, mainly as a result of fabric supply problems. The trousers were introduced in 1907 and were also coarse field grey. These were worn with natural leather marching boots (M1866). In the front line, however, once trench warfare got underway, cloth puttees were worn along with ankle boots.

Königslager

This is another shot that was taken in a training camp shortly before the war. It depended on which part of Germany the soldiers' unit was related to that determined the waist belt. From 1909 it was made in natural leather with a rectangular buckle plate. It usually showed the state badge, a motto and wreath. The standard type had the motto *gott mit uns* – 'God is with us'. Württemberg units had the motto *furchtlos und trew* – 'Fearless and Faithful', Bavarians had *in treue fest* (Steadfast in Loyalty) and Saxons had *provident iae memor* (Remembering God's Care).

Men are queuing for their rations here, which are being served from a field kitchen. The soldiers were issued either an M1887 or M1910 mess tin. This was originally made in aluminium but by October 1914 these were now being made from galvanized tin plate or steel plate and invariably they were painted black. A field grey version was introduced in November 1914 and a field grey steel plate in June 1915. The men also had, at least originally, the M1893 water bottle. This was made of aluminium and had a grey/brown felt cover and a leather strap. A new version was introduced in November 1906 and a tin plate version in October 1914, with yet another variation in June 1915, which was a tin plate bottle in a field grey, waterproof cotton cover.

Three German women are featured in this photograph. They are probably land workers. During the war around 1.6 million German women joined the workforce and many of them worked on the land and in factories, but also for public transport, the post office and in the numerous government departments. The Munitions of Work Act (1915) placed all munitions factories in Germany under the control of the government and some 700,000 German women were employed in such work.

Königslager

This is another shot in one of the training camps shortly before the war, when all German men aged between seventeen and twenty-two were called up to the regular army. From then on men would either join the reserve, effectively for front-line service, or the *Landwehr* for rear area service. Even the *Landsturm* was called out on 15 August 1914 and this would mean that the men still serving in the *Landsturm*, even if they were older than forty-five years would remain in uniform for the duration of the war.

This photograph was taken in Rethel in France, some 36km to the north-east of Reims. Rethel fell to the Germans very early on in the First World War and in fact it remained in German hands until 6 November 1918. The area was clearly an important strategic position, as in August 1914 after the fall of the last French fortress north of Verdun, Longwy, the frontier area had collapsed. French and British troops were falling back. The French 3rd and 4th Armies were unable to make a stand. The Germans forced the River Aisne at Rethel on 28–29 August. This meant that the Allies had to abandon Reims and Chalons.

Chapter Two

Preparing for Battle

Back in the 1890s Field Marshal Alfred von Schlieffen, the Chief of the German General Staff, began examining Germany's potential strategic problem. As a central European power, in the event of war Germany was likely to face a conflict on two fronts. His solution was to deal an overwhelming blow against France with the bulk of the German army, whilst leaving a smaller holding force to contain the Russians. Schlieffen's plan was to entice the French towards the Rhine and then to swing through Belgium and Northern France, pass to the south of Paris, cross the River Seine and effectively pin the entire French army against the fortresses in Lorraine and Switzerland. In order to achieve this Schlieffen believed that they needed a ratio of 7:1 in their favour of men.

The plan and the advantage had been severely diluted by 1914. As it was, the Germans did indeed strike through Belgium, but the French launched their own offensive in Alsace Lorraine. The original Schlieffen plan began to fall apart; instead of passing west of Paris they were passing to the east and the German's flank was exposed to the defensive lines around Paris. The French moved to protect their capital and to face the Germans. Preparations were also under way to strike against the flank and rear of the German forces.

On the morning of 4 September 1914 the French 6th Army was poised to strike. The German 1st Army swung west to meet them. This opened a huge gap between their 1st and 2nd Armies, which were already under severe pressure from the French. The British Expeditionary Force, along with the French 5th Army, entered the gap.

On 9 September, to avoid disaster, the German 1st and 2nd Armies began to withdraw, closely followed by the Allies. The Germans threw up lines of trenches on the River Aisne. What had begun as a fluid war was now beginning to transpose into one of defence and ruinous attacks on dug-in positions.

Within a matter of weeks, a 500-mile battle line had been drawn, running from the Swiss frontier to the North Sea. The trench lines were not yet as sophisticated as they would become. In places opposing armies faced one another at a distance of no more than 10 metres, but in others it was as much as 500 metres. These narrow strips of land would become the battlefields, as the trench lines became more and more sophisticated and elaborate. In fact, by the winter of 1916 the Hindenburg Line, for example, had three lines of double trenches protected by belts of barbed wire, some of which were as much as 100 metres thick.

This is a German infantry battalion, arrayed on a field awaiting inspection by senior officers. Note the presence of the band in the centre of the photograph and, behind them, horse-drawn transports and artillery. The soldiers are wearing helmets rather than field caps. This improved head protection was brought in by the beginning of 1915. The steel helmet was designed to provide basic protection, but its design was limited by the position of the backpack and the fact that the soldier had to aim his rifle. It did not give the men protection from direct small arms fire. In fact it was calculated that the helmet would have to weigh 6kg to achieve this. It took until July 1916 for 300,000 helmets to be issued. The German troops at Verdun and the Somme were supplied first, then the rest of the troops on the Western Front were kitted out, followed by those on the Eastern Front. As the war continued, troops would camouflage their helmets using sacking, paint and mud. It was not until 1918 that the distinctive paint camouflage, or lozenge pattern, was brought in. It is believed that around 7.5 million steel helmets were produced by the Germans during the war.

A German infantry unit is being inspected by senior officers in this photograph. It is believed that the uniformed officer with the white beard is in fact Theobald von Bethmann Hollweg (1856–1921). He served as the Chancellor of Germany between 1909 and 1917. Hollweg was the son of a Prussian official and the grandson of a prominent law scholar. He was one of those that urged Austria to take a tough stance against Serbia following the assassination of Franz Ferdinand. However, it does appear that he was against a war and wanted some kind of solution. He also wanted to maintain reasonable relations with Great Britain. He was considered to be something of a moderate, and although he was not in the German army, he was given the honorary rank of general and would certainly wear the uniform for formal occasions. He desperately tried to keep the United States of America out of the war, and after they did enter the war in 1917 he was forced to resign.

Theobald von Bethmann Hollwegg is taking the salute in this photograph. After studying law at Strasbourg, Leipzig and Berlin, Bethmann Hollwegg joined the civil service. He became the Prussian Minister of the Interior in 1905 and then State Secretary at the Imperial Office of the Interior in 1907. He replaced Prince Bernhard von Boulow as German Chancellor in July 1909.

This photograph, along with the others in this group, appears to have been taken no earlier than late-1915, largely on account of the widespread wearing of steel helmets. Note also that the visiting senior officers are also wearing field grey field service uniforms, rather than dress uniforms, which suggests that these photographs were taken close to the front, just prior to the unit being deployed. It was commonplace, particularly in the early months of the war, for many senior officers to be wearing obsolete uniforms. Many of them had not been that active in the years before the war broke out. In fact Hindenburg himself left for operations on the Eastern Front wearing an obsolete uniform of the 3rd Guards Regiment.

This is another shot of von Bethmann Hollwegg inspecting the troops. Note that two of the officers in the group are wearing *Pickelhaube* helmets with covers. The leather version of this helmet, introduced in 1895, would be worn in the field with a standard M1892 helmet cover. By 1914 this was replaced with a fade resistant cover in grey. Also interesting in this photograph is the apparent use of covers on a number of the troops' helmets, as well as that of one of the officers. Regimental numbers would usually be stencilled onto the front of the helmet in red paint. By August 1914 this had been changed to green paint and by the end of that year the stencilling was usually avoided to reduce visibility. It may be that the troops were told to cover their regimental number, as on close inspection the practice appears to be widespread amongst the rank and file. It is also clear that the photograph has not been doctored in any way by an official censor.

Four men in their field uniforms are featured in this photograph, with Brandenburg style cuffs. In theory their service trousers were designed to match the colour of their jacket. They would be piped in red for infantry and green for *Jager* units. In practice, however, the soldiers would wear stone grey trousers, and many reservists would wear grey, brown or a variety of other colours. It was the officers that would wear the more exaggerated trousers, but they were told in 1915 to keep to the standard width and cut.

A typical scene in a French or Belgian town, with German soldiers looking on as a motorised convoy passes through. On close inspection we can see that some of those in the back of the lead truck are in fact captured French soldiers. They are wearing their *Adrian* steel helmets. These were named after General August Louis Adrian and this was the first pattern steel helmet adopted by the French and issued as standard in 1915. It was made in four parts; the peak, neck, bowl and comb. It had a full leather liner and a leather chinstrap. Once again it had been introduced in order to help reduce head wounds. It was made of mild steel and quite effective against shrapnel. Around 3 million were produced, and like the German equivalent they did not provide a great deal of protection against bullets. It was still being worn by French troops in the Second World War, and in fact a version was still being used by the French police during the 1970s.

This is a good shot of the German infantry unit posing for the camera in a field behind the enemy lines. Note to the left of the photograph there are stacked arms and backpacks. It appears that these men are in full marching order, with their packs, folded greatcoats and ammunition pouches. The majority of the men appear to be wearing long marching boots, rather than ankle boots. Normally each man would have a waist belt and backpack with support straps, he would carry rifle ammunition pouches on each front hip and also carry a bayonet strapped to a spade behind his left hip. In addition to his backpack he would have a shelter quarter, a greatcoat and a canteen, all on his upper back. On his lower back he would carry a gas mask case, a bread bag and a water bottle. Usually the backpack and support straps were taken off for assault orders. The soldier would then wear his greatcoat, shelter quarter and canteen strapped in a horseshoe-shaped roll across his left shoulder.

This is a good shot that shows the vulnerability of the Schneider CA1. With the protruding overhang at the front of the tank it was relatively easy for the tank to tip into trenches or shell holes and get firmly stuck. The tank was originally designed to get over the stalemate of the trenches. Eventually the French would create twenty units, but by 1918, with around 400 having been built, it was replaced by the newer Renault FT17. The Italians had planned to produce at least 1,500 of them for themselves, but after testing one of the vehicles the proposed production run was abandoned. Amazingly one of the Schneider CA1s is still in running condition at the French Musée des Blindés at Saumur, making it the oldest running tank in the world.

This photograph shows an abandoned British tank. The tank appears to be a Mark V, which was a natural development of the Mark I that had entered service in August 1916, being deployed for the first time on 15 September. Note that it has a strong rhomboid shape, giving it a low centre of gravity and extremely long tracks. This was designed specifically to cope with the mud and wide trenches. It also had side-mounted 6pdr guns and a pair of machine guns, with a further two that could be removed on the front and rear.

This is another shot of the stricken British tank, with German infantry giving it a close inspection. The tank had a crew of eight; four of the men were gunners, two handled the gears and in addition there was a driver and a commander. Interestingly, the British decided to create a male and female version of this tank. The male versions had the 6pdr guns and the female versions were just armed with machine guns. Inside the tank there was a large crew space, which was dominated by cordite, carbon monoxide and other gases. Some of the crewmembers actually lost consciousness due to these gases. It was incredibly difficult to steer, the two tracks had variable speed, and generally it never moved any faster than walking pace.

The remains of a fallen soldier. There were literally thousands of unburied bodies along the front lines. In the Somme area alone some 200,000 were killed, and most of these were only buried in shallow graves. The constant churning of the earth by artillery fire would exhume the remains, leaving them scattered and in plain view. This also encouraged black and brown rats. The brown ones could grow to the size of a domestic cat and were partial to human flesh. The soldiers on each side of the conflict spent fruitless hours attempting to kill off the rats but this was almost universally ineffective, as a pair of rats could produce around 900 offspring in a year.

This photograph shows a jumble of charred remnants of an unidentifiable aircraft. Since the majority of the aircraft were built from wood and canvas, they were not only extremely fragile should they crash-land, but they were also highly susceptible to fire. As can be seen in the photograph little remained of this aircraft, except for part of the undercarriage, some wiring and a small section of the propeller.

More unidentifiable human remains; note the fragment of barbed wire. With stalemate, the war on the Western Front became one of attrition. Waves of men would be slaughtered in a matter of minutes by concentrated machine-gun fire. It seemed to matter very little that the enemy entrenchments had been pulverised by artillery fire before an attack. The enemy always had the capacity to bring up reserves, reman the trenches and pour devastating fire back onto the attackers. It was not just machine guns, rifle fire, grenades and artillery shells that caused huge casualties, however. The Germans introduced gas in 1915, causing a mad dash to provide gas masks. Lung irritants such as chlorine were also used and others were simply designed to irritate the eyes. Eventually the most lethal mustard gas was brought in. This blistered the skin and caused the lungs to foam.

Einschläge schwerer Granaten.

This photograph is captioned '*Einschläge schwerer Granaten*', meaning 'the result or impact of heavy grenades'. Both sides used grenades. Initially they were made from empty food cans. The British used an oval-shaped grenade that broke into nearly fifty pieces when it exploded. The Germans used a stick grenade, which was designed to give them a longer throwing distance. The typical stick grenade had a five second fuse. They were considered to be offensive weapons rather than be used in a defensive situation. To use them the soldier would have to un-tape the pull cord from the base of the handle. They would then tug at the cord, which activated a friction ignition, lighting the fuse. There were of course modifications to this weapon over the course of the war, including a variant that exploded on impact. The Germans also used egg-shaped grenades, as well as rifle grenades.

The shattered remains of a shelled village are featured in this photograph. A prime example of the damage done to villages is Fleury, which is to the north-east of Verdun. It was completely destroyed during the First World War and it was never rebuilt. In 1913 just over 400 people lived in Fleury. It first came under shellfire on the morning of 21 February 1916. The villagers were evacuated to Bras-sur-Meuse. On 24 February the Germans captured Fort Douaumont, and by May the village was in ruins and part of the front line. Incredibly, between June and August that year the village, or what remained of it, changed hands sixteen times. The village was bombed once again on 23 June 1916; amongst the shells were gas rounds. The Germans also deployed flamethrowers in the desperate struggle for the ruins. The French retook the ruins on 18 August, by which time the houses had crumbled into the streets and gardens, and everywhere there were bodies. A chapel was built in the late 1970s to commemorate the village. It was one of nine obliterated villages close to Verdun that were never rebuilt and still stands as a memorial.

German soldiers are loading bodies onto a horse-drawn cart here. The scale of death in the First World War was unprecedented; thousands were buried on the battlefields or in communal graves. Many were actually buried where they had fallen. In time this would make identifying individuals incredibly difficult. Graves and burial grounds near the front were invariably obliterated by subsequent fighting and original grave markers were lost. There would eventually be huge numbers of missing individuals. According to the German War Graves Agency at least 80,000 German soldiers killed in Flanders alone cannot be accounted for. At the Arras memorial to the missing there are the names of 34,725 British soldiers missing in action. War graves are still being found. This is despite the fact that the battlefields were cleared of bodies, equipment and ammunition. Some of the dead have remained undiscovered for over ninety years. As late as 2007 the remains of hundreds of British and Commonwealth troops were found near Fromelles in France. It is believed that they were buried there by the Germans after a major battle between 19 and 20 July 1916. Although the site of the graves was marked they had remained undiscovered for decades. It has recently been decided that DNA samples would be taken from the remains to help identify the bodies that are believed to be both British and Australian.

This photograph shows a hastily dug trench on the edge of woodland. Note the rifles laying in firing positions along-side the crouched soldier to the right of the photograph. He is the only man in shot that is wearing a steel helmet; the others are in more relaxed poses and wearing field caps. This is a fairly newly dug trench, as it shows little sign of mud or reinforcement. It is just deep enough for men to crouch or crawl along. Normally the trenches would be built in zigzags. There were two main reasons for this; the first was to absorb the impact of shell blasts if they landed directly in the trench. The second reason was to prevent the enemy, if they had taken a section of trenches, from being able to fire straight along the trench line. The zigzag pattern also had the advantage of providing defensive points, as the enemy would have to fight their way around each corner.

Flämmenwerfer

This is a German flamethrower in action. The Germans deployed *flammenwerfers* as early as October 1914. It was used to great effect, using portable *flammenwerfer* on 30 July 1915 at Hooge in Flanders during an attack on British positions. Over the course of two days nearly 800 British troops were killed by this weapon. It is believed that at least 650 flamethrower attacks were launched by the Germans over the course of the war. After testing the weapon the British abandoned its use. The French tried to develop their version of the portable flamethrower, which was used in the period 1917–18.

German soldiers are picking their way through a shattered village in this shot. Note the two German soldiers in the foreground, in what remains of a trench. Munitions are still being found in northern France. In the village of Coucy-les-Epps, to the north of Reims, a German First World War munitions dump, consisting of nearly 1,700 artillery shells, weighing 30 tons, was found in November 2010. The shells were discovered just a metre below the ground, in a villager's back garden. Some twenty-six bomb experts were brought in to clear the cache, and the 450 inhabitants of the village were evacuated. The shells were moved to remote sites and then destroyed.

German soldiers are standing on the remnants of a dugout, which has received a direct hit from artillery shells. It appears that this partially buried shelter was constructed from logs and corrugated iron. In some cases wood was not available to reinforce trench walls so sandbags were used. Bunkers such as this one were constructed at regular intervals along the trench lines. These would provide radio rooms and sleeping quarters. Some command posts were dug three storeys deep. In theory, it would take around six hours for 450 men to create 250 metres of trenching. Entrenching would be the usual method, but this would expose the men to enemy fire. Sapping could also be used, which would mean digging the ends of the trench first and working inwards. As an alternative, tunnelling could be employed, and the earth overhead would be removed once the line had been created.

This is an overturned German artillery piece, possibly a 105mm Howitzer. Artillery was the biggest killer on the Western Front, arguably accounting for around 70 per cent of all casualties. Despite this, artillery did not always have the desired effect. In July 1917, over a period of fourteen days, the British fired nearly 4.3 million shells at German defences in the Passchendaele area. Despite the intense bombardment, the Germans were still able to mow down British troops as they attempted to overwhelm their lines. At Messines the previous month, the British had concentrated guns against the German lines; they had the equivalent of one gun to every 7 metres of German trench line. They bombarded the Germans for seventeen days, firing the equivalent of 5.5 tons against every 1 metre of the enemy front.

Shattered trees are flanking the bank of a muddy river in France here. One of the major problems with digging trenches was the frequently high water-table. It would mean that the trenches were often flooded and were prone to collapse. Fresh water, however, was a major problem; there was no access to fresh running water. Most of the water courses had been severely polluted either by human waste or by dead bodies. This meant that dysentery was common. Many soldiers on both sides died from exposure in the cold and wet conditions; the trenches were often well below zero in the winter and men would have to wade around in water up to their waists. Many lost toes or fingers to frostbite.

The churned landscape and uprooted, overturned trees are depicted in this photograph. Established trenches would have duckboards at the bottom of the trench line. In theory, mud and water would be restricted to the area of the trench underneath the duckboard, but in reality, if the water-table was high, or there had been heavy rain, then the trenches became a sea of mud and water. In some cases the mud was so deep that men had to stand on barrels. The mud also brought other dangers; there was a resilient bacterium that lived in the soil of Flanders. If this got into a wound then it would swell and men would often die from the infections. It was also not unknown for men to literally disappear in the mud. As we can see in this photograph, a huge crater has been filled with mud and water. Hazards such as this would claim not only men but also horses.

22 Musterh. Stellungskrieg. Graben unter zersch. Bäumen

This photograph is captioned 'trench warfare under the trees'. The soldier is cleaning what appears to be his G98 rifle. It has a Mauser self-cocking breech and had a barrel of 74cm long. To load the rifle the bolt was pulled back, and when the bolt was closed the mechanism was cocked and the first cartridge was in the chamber. It had an elongated stock and was originally designed to use a 52cm long bayonet. In practice, however, a 37cm, broader bayonet was often used. The rifle went into mass production in 1900. By the time the war broke out in 1914 not all of the troops had been issued with this new weapon. In comparison to the British short magazine Lee Enfield, it was longer and more difficult to use in the confined spaces of the trenches. It also only had a five-round magazine. Eventually a twenty-five-round trench magazine was designed, but this was never produced in sufficient numbers. By 1918 work had begun on another weapon, which had a twenty-five-round magazine and was designed specifically as a trench and close combat rifle. This was known as the *Mausergewehr18*.

The gruesome remains of a dead soldier, who is lying on the battlefield. In Belgium alone, there were 128 German military burial sites. These ranged in size from single burials beside roads, canals and ditches or in fields and woods, to large groups, with over 3,000 bodies. Many of the individual graves and cemetery sites were destroyed during the course of the war. In 1925 the Belgian government reached an agreement with the Germans to begin the exhumation of German graves. Ultimately two cemeteries were redeveloped to create official burial sites. After the Second World War collecting cemeteries were established at Langemarck-Nord (44,234 burials), Vladslo (25,638 burials) and Menen (47,864 burials). The so-called Comrades Grave at Langemarck-Nord was established as the internment place for all unidentified German dead. There are still smaller cemeteries, one at Zeebrugge with 173 graves and the other at Hooglede with 8,247 graves.

German soldiers are sheltering in the remains of a bunker that is situated within a heavily shelled, wooded area of the front. The complexity of German trenches became clear when, from around 1916, the Allies started to capture some of these trench lines. Some of the dugouts were as deep as 7 metres underground and some had been reinforced with concrete and had generators for electricity, cookers and anti-gas curtains. The German principle was that of defence in depth, with trench lines a mile or two behind the front that could be used as a fallback position if necessary. One German soldier that was killed near Ypres on 15 April 1915 clearly operated in terrain very similar to that shown in this photograph. Their trench line was just 60 metres from the British lines and behind them, around 600 metres to the rear, was a small, wooded valley. He described the trees and bushes as being shredded by shelling, and that each tree was peppered with bullets. All around the area there were huge shell holes with bodies lying scattered, several of which were the corpses of comrades that they had buried. The pine wood was almost completely destroyed by shelling. They used the tree tops to help reinforce their defensive lines. To make the trenches a little more like home the men would carve names into the dugouts.

This photograph shows an overturned artillery piece that is lying amongst the blasted remains of a gun emplacement. Note the cut wood that would have formed part of the entrenchment in which the gun would have operated. This appears to be a 100mm canon or similar, which was used as a long-range artillery piece by the Germans. It was used for counter-battery fire and for bringing down fire on key positions, such as road junctions, to the enemy's rear. The M04 version had a range of just over 10km, the M14 a range of 13km.

This is another shattered German artillery piece. This time we can clearly see the wooden gun platform, and installed mechanism to reduce the recoil of the artillery piece when it was fired. Again, this artillery piece appears to have taken an almost direct hit. It has shattered all of the wooden parts of the gun's chassis and has churned up the entrenchment, leaving its remains exposed. Most of the German guns were painted in field grey. From around 1917, in order to camouflage themselves from enemy aircraft, additional colours were added over the top of the field grey, including sand, green and brown. In reality, however, the colours consisted of a medium green, a dark nutty brown, an ochre sand colour and a red-brown. There was also black used as part of the camouflage scheme.

This is an interesting photograph, as it shows shattered trench lines, barbed wire and ruined houses, yet the group of soldiers do not appear to be either armed or particularly concerned about coming under fire from the enemy. This may be a former front line, now used as a rest area. There were also occasions when there were unofficial ceasefires. One German soldier at Verdun, in December 1916, described the situation whenever there was heavy rain. Both the Germans and the French suffered from flooded trenches, and in fact the trench lines became so muddy and waterlogged that they were almost rivers. The men would sit opposite one another during an unofficial ceasefire, baling out water and constructing drainage ditches.

This photograph shows a huge crater, which must be upwards of 8–10m deep. Huge craters such as these were created by detonating underground mines. At the battle of Messines in June 1917 the British dug twenty-two mineshafts under the German lines, all along the Messines Ridge. At 0310 hours on 7 June they were to detonate all of the mines, which was to be followed by an overwhelming infantry attack. The Germans attempted to countermine and there was hand-to-hand fighting underground. As it was, nineteen of the underground mines were detonated and it has been estimated that some 10,000 German soldiers were killed. The British then launched nine infantry divisions, supported by artillery, tanks and gas attacks. All of the objectives were taken, but the Germans counter-attacked on 8 June, albeit to no avail, leaving the Messines salient in Allied hands.

This photograph is captioned 'Laufgraben' or 'approach trench'. Approach trenches were designed to provide protection to the soldiers between the rear and front lines of defensive positions. Effectively they were communication trenches. In some cases the sides of the approach trenches were reinforced with brushwood and wattle hurdles. In the Somme in 1916 the German trenches were deep and solidly built. They were interconnected with other trenches. The approach trenches were used to bring up supplies, reinforcements and ammunition. The Germans would also incorporate farms and other buildings, linking them with a maze of underground work. Each and every position was designed to make it as difficult as possible to either approach it, or to overwhelm it.

This photograph shows a machine-gun team, who are deployed at the edge of a wood. This is probably an MG08, which was the standard machine gun used by the Germans. They would normally set up two defensive positions. In trench systems the machine guns were given deep dugouts, and were only brought out when the trenches were not being bombarded. It was typical to set up machine-gun posts at the edges of woodland, or in other cover. They would be supported by infantry, who could also operate as replacement gunners. The machine-gun crews were supposed to have at least 11,500 rounds to hand. The guns would fire routine volleys to check ranges, and they would be equipped with four spare barrels, a water supply and the crewmembers would have side arms, grenades and a flare pistol.

Chapter Four

The Enemy

Although combatants would clearly see the enemy at a distance during their normal trench warfare duties, the only time they would actually see the enemy close-up would be as a prisoner of war. During the nineteenth century efforts were made to improve the treatment of prisoners of war. The Brussels Conference in 1874 agreed that prisoners should be treated in a humane way, but there were no final agreements. The 1907 Hague Convention dealt directly with the treatment of prisoners of war. Men had to be entitled to prisoner of war status, and to qualify, they must have been engaged in military operations and be part of a fixed chain of command. This led to grey areas, which made it difficult for those that did not wear uniform and could be classed as saboteurs, spies or *francs-tireurs* (irregulars).

Over the course of the First World War some 8 million men were taken prisoner. The vast majority of countries adhered to the Hague Convention. This meant that men had a far better chance of surviving their imprisonment. In one engagement alone, at Tannenberg, on the Eastern Front, from 23 August to 30 August 1914 over 90,000 Russians were taken prisoner. In fact Germany held as many as 2.5 million prisoners during the war. The Germans were especially criticised for their treatment of Russian prisoners, although there were instances of poor treatment of French, British and American troops taken on the Western Front. By the end of the First World War there were upwards of 140,000 British prisoners held in Germany. Collectively, some 264,000 prisoners of all nationalities had been released to the west by early December 1918.

Although the bulk of western prisoners were released shortly after the armistice in 1918, German and Austrian prisoners of war continued to be held, and many were used as forced labourers. A considerable number were held in France until at least 1920.

Typical experience of a British soldier captured by the Germans, even as late as 1918, is that of Arthur Beaumont, who joined the machine-gun corps. He was involved in an attack launched on 21 March 1918. The British forces had made reasonable progress, but then the Germans counter-attacked and in the ensuing chaos Beaumont was captured. Beaumont and the other prisoners made their way east, being fed *en route* with coffee, a slice of bread and bowls of vegetable soup. They marched towards Guise, which is due east from Amiens. The men were marching with thousands of captured French troops. Beaumont was not able to tell his parents that he was still alive, and in fact his mother received a telegram on 2 May 1918 informing her of his capture.

Beaumont continued marching east towards Landrecies, close to the Belgian border. They then marched on towards Giessen prisoner of war camp in Bavaria. Beaumont described it as a well-ordered camp that had been in operation since 1914. He was put to work in a mine and fed coffee and bread each morning, after which he was expected to load blocks of iron stone onto coal mine trucks. After two weeks Beaumont was sent to a smelting factory and then his third job was at a tannery near Frankfurt. Eventually Beaumont and the others received word of the armistice and they left Germany via Saarbrucken, then Metz, before travelling on to Calais.

Beaumont finally returned home to Cambridgeshire on 14 December 1918. He was one of five sons; one of them had been killed in 1915, another in 1918, a third had been discharged after being wounded, the fourth had fallen ill, and Arthur himself, had been taken prisoner. He went on to become a parish vicar and died on 6 July 1983.

Gefangene Franzosen. 4. III. 18.

French prisoners of war are standing outside the lecture room in an unnamed prisoner of war camp on 4 March 1918. On 11 November 1918, at the time of the armistice, there were 477,800 French prisoners in German care. Repatriation took some time but they were all back in France by January 1919. Huge numbers of French prisoners had been taken during the fighting; at the fortified city of Maubeuge 40,000 prisoners had been captured. In some of the camps the men received harsh treatment, but usually the officers' camps had a more relaxed regime. In some of the camps there was no heating, beds or healthcare, notable amongst which were those at Minden, Lechfeld and Niedrzwehren. Over time, crowded conditions led to outbreaks of tuberculosis and typhus. In 1915 some 2,000 French prisoners died when typhus broke out at Kassel and Wittenberg. News of the harsh treatment in some of the camps was met by a swift German reaction. They cut the food rations, prevented mail from being sent or received, and many French prisoners were sent to special camps that had been set up in Lithuania. The Germans later claimed that this was a reaction against threats of reprisals against German prisoners.

Gefangene Franzosen. 10.XII.17.

This is another shot of French prisoners of war, this time an earlier date of 10 December 1917. By 1916 around 300,000 French had been made prisoners of war. Officers were exempt from having to work, but the bulk of them worked in the fields or in factories. At Essen around 30,000 worked in the Krupp armaments factories. There were improvements in the daily life and conditions under which prisoners were kept as a result of the Berne accords of 1917. These took effect in May 1918.

French troops were also kept as work details behind the front lines. Here they tended to work on road building projects, or to help improve the railway links. Large numbers of French prisoners worked close to the front at Aisen, Champagne and Verdun between 1916 and 1917. It is believed that around 4,000 French prisoners died on French soil that was German occupied. It was not just French soldiers that were rounded up, however. Around 180,000 civilian men, women and children were sent to camps. It is believed that around 30,000 of this number died. Many of them were conscripted by force to work on road and rail projects. Effectively these were civilian labour battalions, or *zivilarbeiterbataillon*. Men between the ages of fourteen and sixty were required to do hard labour from April 1916, and by 1917 this had been expanded to women between fifteen and forty-five years. Those that caused problems were sent to work in mines, or the penal colony that had been set up at Sedan.

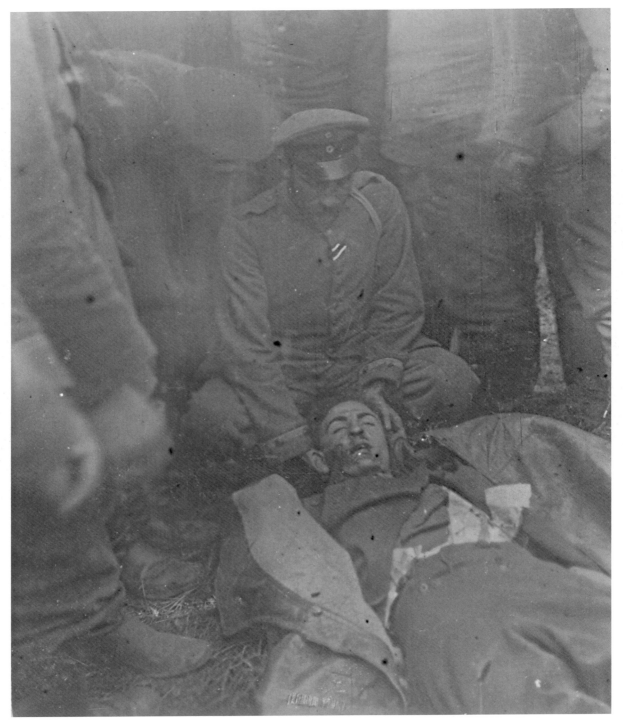

A dying German airman. He is wearing a pilot badge on the right lapel of his jacket, which can be seen more clearly in the next photograph. The French pilot Rene Fonck claimed 126 kills but is only credited with seventy-five of them. Manfred von Richthofen claimed to have shot down around eighty enemy aircraft. The Germans, particularly on the Western Front were invariably outnumbered in the air. They built around 50,000 aircraft, whereas the British and French produced 125,000. A great deal of the action took place over the Germans' own trenches. They tended to react to Allied attacks rather than launch offensives of their own. This meant that the Germans required less fuel and less flying time. It was also the case that many of their pilots, dead, injured, or safe, could be recovered.

The same unnamed German pilot is seen here, who now appears to have died from his injuries. There were other notable German aces, such as Ernst Udet, who was the leading surviving German ace of the war, as well as the youngest. He was still only twenty-two in 1918, but nonetheless he was able to claim sixty-two victories. By May 1918 the air war had been won by the Allies. Udet described the Allied air fleets overflying German positions as appearing to look like locusts. In fact Udet admitted that whenever an Allied aircraft was forced down, he would try to land near it, and strip the aircraft of any instruments or equipment, as well as pumping gasoline out of the tank.

British prisoners of war, in an unnamed camp, are shown here. This photograph was probably taken towards the latter stages of the war. Upwards of 170,000 British and Commonwealth troops were taken by Germany and their allies as prisoners during the First World War. The last known surviving Allied soldier that was captured on the Western Front died on Christmas Eve 2005. Professor Harold Lawton joined the 4th Battalion of the East Yorkshire Regiment and was sent into the line at Bethune in March 1918. He arrived at a time of chaos, and he and six others found themselves cut off when the Germans infiltrated the Allied lines. Lawton and the others were captured and sent to Lille, where they were imprisoned in a fortress that became known as The Black Hole of Lille. Lawton and the others were reported missing, possibly dead. After Lille they were sent to Limburg in Westphalia, and then on to a prisoner of war camp at Minden.

This is a close-up of some of the soldiers in the same camp as that shown in the previous photograph. From the look of the soldiers they all appear to have been recently captured. During the Second World War, Harold Lawton spent his time lecturing British and Allied troops about how to blend in, in France, should they find themselves cut off or having escaped from a German prisoner of war camp. At the age of 99 Lawton was awarded the French Legion of Honour. He died at the age of 106 years, and had often described the chaotic nature of his short stay in the trenches. He was also highly critical of the conditions under which the Germans had kept Allied prisoners; the lack of food, space, and the poor treatment of men who were wounded or had dysentery.

This is a downed Airco DH4, which was a British two-seater biplane bomber that was used for daylight operations. The aircraft first entered service in March 1917. This particular aircraft is identified as being A7661, which was flown by Second-Lieutenant Norman Harold Thackrah (according to AIR76/499) and Lieutenant Walter George Fluke (according to AIR76/165) of 55 Squadron. This aircraft was shot down on 24 March 1918 by *Vizefeldwebel* Fritz Schwarz of *Jagdstaffel* 33. This formation (*Jagdstaffel* 33) was formed in December 1916 and was barely in action when this incident took place. The German squadron was almost certainly based in France at the time, and they would have been flying Fokker DRIs, a German triplane. This aircraft came into service in the spring of 1918. We know little about Schwarz, but what we do know is that his aircraft crashed on 15 August 1918 and he was killed. There are references to Second-Lieutenant Thackrah in post-First World War Royal Flying Corps records, which seem to suggest that he at least survived the encounter on 24 March, and almost undoubtedly became a prisoner of war.

Engl. flieger abgesch. 24. III. 1918.

This photograph is dated 24 March 1918 and clearly marked are two crosses, identifying who we believe to be Second-Lieutenant N.H. Thackrah, to the extreme left of the photograph, and Lieutenant W.G. Fluke, seated in the rear of the car. We can see from Fluke's uniform that he is wearing an observer's badge on his left front tunic. The caption reads 'English fliers set out', which must refer to the fact that the aircraft came down close to the front line and then, as prisoners of war, the two fliers were taken to a rear area, to a camp. The photograph was taken outside a German commandant's office. Although we have been unable to research more about Lieutenant W.G. Fluke, it is apparent that N.H. Thackrah survived the war. There is mention of him in the *London Gazette*, dated 28 October 1924, as a Flying Officer that had been transferred from a Class A to a Class C.

Chapter Five

The Aircraft

With trench warfare firmly established, the traditional role of cavalry had been lost. Both sides began to become increasingly reliant on aircraft to carry out reconnaissance. An integral part of this was photo reconnaissance, which aimed to reveal the positions of enemy trenches, works and troop build-ups. Naturally, these reconnaissance aircraft needed protection, thus the single-seater fighter was developed. From around 1915, on the Western Front, both sides vied to control the air over the battlefields. There were rapid improvements in aircraft, tactics and pilot skills.

The two-seater observation aircraft remained the most important feature of the aerial war. It was, therefore, the case that the majority of air combat took place literally over the trenches. Comparatively speaking, there was very little strategic bombing; this of course would change markedly in the Second World War. There were, of course, notable exceptions to this rule; airships were still deployed, particularly the Zeppelin, which launched a number of offensives against Britain. Later the Germans would deploy the Gotha bomber and launch a series of strategic strikes.

Initially the combat aircraft over the trenches suffered from a lack of effective fire-power; however, in 1915 the French developed a system by which a forward-firing machine gun could literally shoot through the propellers. In April 1915 Roland Garros, a French pilot, shot down five enemy aircraft using this new system. Unfortunately Garros was shot down, which allowed the Germans to develop their own version of the forward-firing machine gun. Their new system would revolutionize combat in the air and for a time it gave the Germans the decisive edge. In response, the Allies began deploying their aircraft in large formations, to provide all-round protection.

By 1916 the Germans had brought in a new, single-seater fighter, the Albatross DIII, and had reorganized their fighter units into hunting groups. In April 1917 the British alone lost 150 aircraft to these new German formations.

The air war continued, with ever greater numbers of aircraft deployed in the skies above the trenches. In June 1917, under the command of Manfred von Richthofen, the Germans created four fighter wings. These aimed to ensure local air superiority, but over the same period of time new Allied fighters were coming on stream, including the Sopwith Camel and the SE5. It was these aircraft that would give the Allies air supremacy for the remainder of the war.

Any airman that could claim ten or more kills was deemed an ace. In fact, around thirty Allied or German pilots could claim forty or more kills.

For the most part, by the second half of the First World War, German air units would react to Allied attacks, rather than launch their own offensives. With the Allied aircraft coming in at altitudes of 13,000 feet or more (particularly bombers), the Germans would need a considerable amount of time to get to that altitude to intercept them. They would receive an alert notice once the Allied aircraft had crossed the German trench line. In most cases they would not be able to engage until the bombers were on their return trip. It is important to remember that there was no early warning system. It could take an aircraft up to thirty minutes to reach an altitude of 15,000 feet.

It would appear that many of the photographs in this part of the album date to around 1917. This year was a particularly bloody year; there had been vicious fighting around Arras, and many of the French squadrons had been withdrawn from the front line in order to reinforce and reorganize them. The British continued to fight on, deploying some 385 fighters against an estimated German fighter force of 114. However, in the April, the British lost a third of their fighters. Incredibly, seventeen and a half hours was the life expectancy of a British pilot.

This is a photograph of a downed Neuport 17. Its tail serial number, N2405, identifies it as belonging to *Escadrille* 506. The aircraft was shot down on 11 February 1917. The Neuport 17 was a natural replacement for the Neuport 11 and it came into service in March 1916. It was also used by the Royal Flying Corps and the Royal Naval Air Service. The Germans captured a number of these and made their own copy; the Siemens-Schucker DI. It only had a short period of success and by mid-1917 it had been replaced by the Spad SVII. The Neuport 17 was a single-seater biplane with a maximum speed of 177km/h and an operational flight time of one and three-quarter hours.

This photograph shows another captured French aircraft. The pilot is standing in the darker coloured uniform, still wearing his leather flight helmet. The aircraft can just be identified as a Neuport 24, which was a development of the Neuport 17. It came into service in the summer of 1917, but by this stage the majority of the French fighter squadrons were actually being equipped with Spad SVIIs, rather than the Neuport 24. The Neuport 24 had an improved fuselage, an aerodynamic shape with rounded wing-tips, as can be seen in the photograph. It had a maximum speed of 187km/h.

This particular aircraft was part of *Escadrille* N89 and was piloted by Henri Durand. He force landed the aircraft at Ommeray, in Lorraine, on 6 January 1918. He had apparently encountered engine trouble after attacking a German balloon near Bourdonna in the Lothringen area, which is to the east of Nancy. Durand was originally reported as killed in action, but he was in fact taken prisoner, as this photograph attests.

Here we have another photograph of Henri Durand, looking rather glum amongst a large group of German soldiers. The French built over 52,000 aircraft during the course of the First World War and it is believed that 8,500 of these were lost, although some of them may have been aircraft that were scrapped, used for spare parts, or simply replaced. It is also believed that the French only ever had slightly less than 5,000 aircraft engaged in front line duties. The vast majority of these were on the Western Front; around 3,200 at any one time. They also had squadrons in Italy, Greece and Serbia. At least another 1,000 were based in the Mediterranean, and along the Channel coast. The French had around 4,500 front line aircraft in June 1918. It is important to remember that aircraft were being replaced at least every five to six months, due to newer aircraft being brought into service.

This is a closer shot of Durand, this time with the wing of his aircraft clearly visible, and showing Type 24 (Neuport) and his aircraft serial number, 5449. He is wearing a dark blue, almost black uniform. We can see the French aviator's badge worn on the right side of his jacket. There were several variations of this badge, which was essentially a laurel circle with a star and wings. Aircraft pilots would have gold wings with gold stars, aviator students and spotters would have silver stars, gunners and bombers would have a single wing and a two-blade propeller in silver, and observers would have a single wing and a gold star.

This particular aircraft is a Neuport 17 belonging to Escadrille N68. It has the serial number 1955. The pilot was named Mdl Blaise Preher, who was apparently forced to land after being attacked by *Leutnant* Slazwedel of *Jasta* 24 in the French 8th Army sector. This is likely to have occurred on 11 April 1917. The most successful Neuport 17 pilot was in fact a Britain; Philip Fullard. He claimed forty victories, flying successively the Neuport 17, 23, and 27. Fullard, a former Norwich City Football Club reserve player, joined the army in 1915. He was transferred to the Royal Flying Corps and was posted to France in April 1917, attached to No. 1 Squadron. His love of football caused him to miss operations at Cambrai in November 1917, when he broke a leg playing in a game and was unable to fly for nearly a year. Fullard was awarded the Military Cross, being cited as having attacked and destroyed four enemy aircraft and engaged in twenty-five other combats. He was then awarded the bar to his cross for destroying eight German aircraft; before receiving the Distinguished Service Order, not only for his duties as a patrol leader, and his gallantry, but also for shooting down fourteen German aircraft and driving another eighteen to the ground, in four months. On one occasion Fullard was attacked by a German two-seater aircraft and had his goggles shot off his face. Fullard survived the war and died at the age of eighty-six in Kent.

This photograph depicts what appears to be a man, or more likely a dummy, being dropped by parachute. As far as the First World War is concerned, parachutes were certainly used by observers escaping from observation balloons. They were static targets, and it was unlikely that the ground crew would be able to winch the balloon down quickly enough. It was not generally considered to be the case that the Germans, or the Austro-Hungarians, thought that parachutes were suitable for fixed wing aircraft. This was certainly the case until at least 1918.

Possibly the first successful use of a parachute by a German pilot took place on 1 April 1918. A pilot called Weimar of *Jasta* 56 was shot down, and his aircraft burst into flames. He baled out using a parachute over Gontelles and became a prisoner of war.

There were several other successful uses by German or Austro-Hungarian pilots, although on a number of occasions parachutes failed to open. One such case occurred on 8 September 1918 when *Jasta* 6's Kurt Blumener's parachute failed to open, as did that of Albert Haussman of *Jasta* 13 on 16 October 1918. It was a hazardous task to bale out of an aircraft. Friedrich 'Fritz' Friedrichs of *Jasta* 10 attempted to parachute, but it got caught on the tailplane, it ripped, and he fell to his death on 15 July 1918.

A two-seater German aircraft is undergoing repairs in this photograph, in what appears to be extremely cold weather conditions. The photograph was probably taken over the winter of 1917 to 1918 and is that of a German *Albatros DIII*. It came into service in December 1916, and it had serious faults. If the radiator in the centre of the upper wing was hit, then the pilot would be scalded. Also there were dangerous failures on the lower wing ribs and leading edge, which on at least one occasion caused the complete failure of the lower right wing. Around 500 of these aircraft were, however, completed, and at the peak some 446 were operating on the Western Front in November 1917. It remained in service all the way through to the end of the war. It is believed that towards the end of August 1918 there were still fifty-four of them operational on the Western Front. The aircraft was particularly effective in the spring of 1917, where it accounted for scores of Allied aircraft.

The smouldering remains of an unidentifiable aircraft are shown here. The only clue that we have to the nationality of the aircraft is the barely visible German Imperial Cross on the tailplane, to the right of the photograph, and directly in front of the line of men. The Germans published their losses on a monthly basis, and from March to September 1918, their losses never fell below 110 per month. In fact in March they lost 164 planes, rising to 185 in May.

The wrecked remains of a German aircraft are shown here. Note the lines of barbed wire extending up the hill where it is possible to see some shelters or emplacements. Originally the German air force was known as the *Die Fliegertruppen des Deutschen Kaiserreiches* (Imperial German Flying Corps). In October 1916 it became known as the *Deutsche Luftstreitkrafte* (German Air Force). Prussia provided the bulk of the squadrons; some sixty-seven of them. Bavaria supported ten, Saxony seven, and Württemberg four. Each of the aircraft was designated a code number, which incorporated the name of the manufacturer, the function of the aircraft, and a Roman numeral, for example, a single-seater, unarmed biplane, but later fighters, were designated with the letter D. The Germans listed some 8,604 aircrew killed, missing, or taken as prisoners of war. Some 7,302 were wounded, and in all they are reckoned to have lost 3,126 aircraft. The German air force was dissolved on 8 May 1920, under the terms of the Treaty of Versailles.

This is another photograph of a downed German aircraft, with soldiers picking through the debris for parts and souvenirs. The man standing in the left foreground appears to have a partial belt of ammunition in his hands. One of the most successful groups was *Jagdgeschwader* I, or *Geschwader Richthofen*. It was often referred to by the Allies as 'Richthofen's Flying Circus'. It was mobilised in June 1917 and the German air force's first fighter wing. Richthofen was killed in action on 21 April 1918, although there is some debate as to how he died. He was apparently in pursuit of Canadian pilot Wilfred Reid May, who would have been Richthofen's eighty-first kill, when he pursued the Sopwith Camel along the Somme Canal. The two aircraft passed over the village of Vaux-sur-Somme when Pilot Arthur Roy Brown of 9 Naval Squadron supposedly shot down Richthofen, receiving a bar to his Distinguished Service Cross as a result. Richthofen's aircraft, a Fokker DR1, banked to the right, and was then seen to crash into the ground. Brown was officially credited with the victory, but new evidence seemed to suggest that a machine gun fired from one of the British trenches actually downed Richthofen's aircraft.

Little remains of this unidentified aircraft, which is captured in this photograph smouldering in the countryside. It may well be that this aircraft was deliberately set on fire, having made a forced landing, as one of the wheels remains firmly rooted in place. Aircraft such as that favoured by Richthofen were triplanes. They were able to make very tight turns, climb quickly, and were deadly against inexperienced pilots. Despite the fact that the Fokker DR1 was relatively uncommon, and in fact only 320 saw service, it is undoubtedly, along with the Sopwith Camel, the most famous aircraft of the First World War. It was first introduced in August 1917 and had a maximum speed of around 165km/h. It had a pair of front firing light machine guns. Richthofen racked up twenty or more kills out of his total of eighty in a DR1. Another pilot, Verner Voss, shot down twenty-one Allied aircraft in around three weeks, before he too was shot down on 23 September 1918. Verner Voss was both a friend and rival to von Richthofen. Voss ran into six SE5s of the Royal Flying Corps 56 Squadron on 23 September, by which time he was approaching fifty kills. Unfortunately for Voss he had encountered an elite unit, comprising of Captain James McCudden (fifty-seven kills), Richard Maybery (twenty-one kills), Geoffrey Bowman (thirty-two kills), Reginald Hoidge (twenty-eight kills), Arthur Rhys-Davids (twenty-three kills), and Keith Muspratt (eight kills). Voss fought alone against them for ten minutes, apparently riddling each of the SE5s with shots. Eventually the British pilots scored hits of their own. Hoidge riddled Voss's Fokker and a round pierced Voss's lungs. Rhys-Davids came in for the kill, emptying two drums of Lewis gun bullets into Voss's triplane. Voss's aircraft smashed into the ground to the north of Frezenberg, Belgium, and only fragments of it were ever recovered. Voss, however, had done quite a lot of damage; both Muspratt and Maybery had to force land. Other aircraft from No. 60 Squadron, which was also engaged, were also badly damaged. Voss is now buried near Ypres in Belgium.

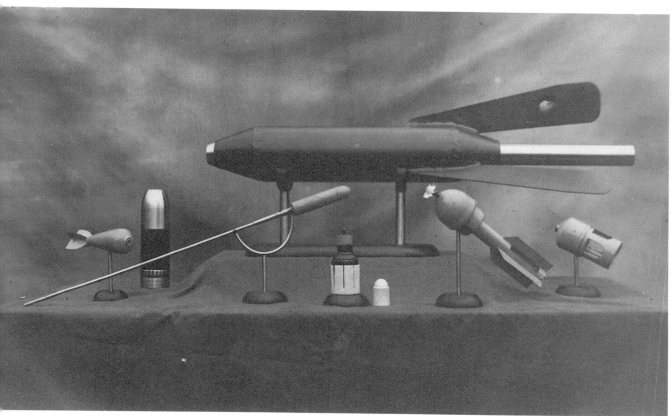

This photograph shows a collection of bombs, and other weapons used by aircraft during the First World War, as well as what appear to be mortar rounds. Many of these bombs were dropped from aircraft by hand, onto the enemy. It would take a great deal of precision and nerve to come in low over enemy positions and drop bombs; with the threat of fire from the ground, as well as the ever-present danger of being intercepted by an enemy aircraft. In late 1915 the British put their first mortar into production. It was a basic 4-inch pipe that used a cylindrical bomb, had a maximum range of 150 metres and had a twenty-five second fuse. The most well known British mortar of the First World War was the Stokes mortar, which was simple and easy to use. It was a smooth metal tube with a base plate and had a bipod mount. The mortar bomb weighed around 4.5kg and an experienced crew could fire twenty-two rounds per minute, with a maximum range of approximately 1,200 metres.

This is another photograph of a selection of aerial weapons (those with the fins) and other projectiles. The Germans used a *Minenwerfer* (mine thrower). They produced these in three different sizes; light, medium and heavy. These were first used on the Western Front, and after successful battlefield deployment went into mass production. At the beginning of the war the Germans had around 150 mortars available to them. Mortar tactics tended to be used against machine-gun posts, sniper positions, or in the case of larger mortars, to cut holes in enemy barbed wire. They tended to be used when it was not practicable to use field artillery.

This appears to be a downed Airco DH4, which came into service with the Royal Flying Corps in March 1917. It was used as a general-purpose two-seater by the Americans in France. The first squadron to adopt the aircraft was No. 55 Squadron and it was originally designed as a two-seater, daytime bomber. It was of wooden construction and the crew of two were separated by the fuel tank. There was a synchronized Vickers machine gun in the nose and the observer had one, or two, Lewis guns mounted on a ring for rear and side protection. The crewmembers communicated using a speaking tube. The DH4 could carry a bomb load of up to 210kg. The Royal Flying Corps and Royal Naval Air Service received a total of 1,499 of the aircraft, and the Americans made the DH4 under license. Some 9,500 were ordered, but only 1,885 arrived in France before the war ended. The aircraft was relatively successful, but by the spring of 1918 production had switched over to the DH9, which was a far less successful aircraft.

Chapter Six

War Damages

Under the terms of the Treaty of Versailles Germany was expected to pay enormous reparations. Considering that the war on the Western Front had been confined to Belgium and parts of France, a staggering 100,000 tons of pure gold was demanded. At the time, it was reckoned to amount to something in the region of £13 billion, or $64 billion (in modern terms $785 billion). The Germans made their final payment on 4 October 2010.

The war had devastated the industrial north-east of France. It was an area that had produced nearly 60 per cent of all of France's steel and 40 per cent of her coal. As the Germans retreated, they destroyed many of the mines in both France and Belgium. France came out of the war with 1.4 million soldiers dead, and overall some 8 million soldiers had been killed, with 7 million disabled during the conflict. A further 15 million had serious injuries as a result. France had lost 10.5 per cent of its active male population and Germany had similarly lost 15.1 per cent.

Belgium had also suffered greatly. Some 25,000 homes and other buildings had been destroyed, and around 20 per cent of the Belgian population had fled west in the wake of the invading German army. The Germans had entered Belgium on 4 August 1914 and around 6,500 civilians were killed.

After 1918 there was an enormous amount of work to be carried out in clearing the battlefields and trying to turn the countryside back to a habitable state. Whole villages, towns, farms, roads and woods had been wiped off the face of the earth. There was the hazardous job of clearing battlefield debris, weapons, ammunition, unexploded bombs and, of course, thousands of soldiers' remains. Some places were

(*Opposite page*) These two photographs were taken in the Thiaucourt region of France. Thiaucourt is in the Lorraine area and is now the location of the St Mihiel American Cemetery and memorial. It contains the remains of over 4,000 US troops, most of who died during the reduction of the German salient of St Mihiel. Also located at Thiaucourt is a German cemetery dating back to the Franco-Prussian War of 1871. Over 11,500 German soldiers lie here, and each of the crosses in the cemetery marks four graves.

On 12 September 1918 American pilots crossed the German lines and flew to the north-east of Thiaucourt. They circled the area and noticed enemy artillery flashes in the Bois de Thiaucourt, they then flew over the stream near the destroyed railway bridge and were shot at by several hidden machineguns. American artillery fire began hitting the Bois de Thiaucourt area. Thiaucourt was considered to be an important railway centre within the St Mihiel salient.

designated to become permanent memorials. The British wanted Ypres to remain in ruins as a memorial but this was rejected.

It is still possible to see the mark of the First World War on the landscape of France and Belgium. Areas are still clearly cratered, and there are many ponds that were former shell holes. Numerous bunkers and strong points can still be seen. On a daily basis objects are still found, including the remains of soldiers. One of the largest craters on the Western Front was caused by a mine that was detonated under German front lines in the Somme on 1 July 1916. It is known as Lochnagar Crater and it is now an official battlefield site.

This photograph shows a wrecked and partially submerged small railway bridge. It is probably on the Toul to Thiaucourt railway. Toul had been important in the Franco-Prussian war, where its defences were used as the base for sixty-four artillery pieces. It surrendered after around 2,400 shells had been fired. It was severely damaged during this war, however, due to its close proximity to Verdun it found itself also part of the St Mihiel salient during the First World War.

This photograph shows what appear to be the shattered walls of a town within the St Mihiel salient. The German defensive positions in the St Mihiel salient were focused around three villages: Vigneulles-les-Hattonchatel, Thiaucourt and Hannonville-sous-les-Cotes. Incredibly, a newspaper in Switzerland had not only published the fact that the American offensive was imminent, but had also noted the time, date, and duration of the barrage that would precede the attack. As it was, the Germans lacked sufficient troops within the salient and ultimately they would take the decision to pull back towards the Hindenburg line.

This is a destroyed railway gun. The best known were those made by Krupp during the First World War. The French were extremely short of heavy field artillery at the beginning of the war and tried to solve the problem by deploying railway guns. They also developed a 520mm Fort Buster, in order to be used against the main German defensive lines. One of them was destroyed during trials, whilst the other was put into storage. It was later captured by the Germans and used against the Russians during the siege of Leningrad.

Here we can see another photograph of the destroyed railway gun. This photograph suggests that this could, in fact be a US made railway gun. A number of these were shipped into France and assembled at Saint Nazaire in August 1918. These weapons were fired at ranges of 27–36km against targets on the German front. Alternatively, this could well be a German 280mm railway gun, which was originally a naval piece and adapted for land service.

Here we see solidly built defensive positions. These are almost certainly the remains of a French built fort from the nineteenth century that were utilized by the French initially, and subsequently by the Germans during the First World War. Straight after the reduction of the St Mihiel salient nine US divisions were brought up to deploy between the Meuse River and the Argonne Forest. To support them they had upwards of 190 tanks, 2,700 artillery pieces and over 800 aircraft. They would work in cooperation with the 4th French Army, which was attempting to make its way west of the Argonne Forest. The infantry assault was launched at 0530 hours on 26 September 1918, with tank support. The US troops made good progress and by the evening of 28 September they had advanced up to 11km.

These two photographs show what is thought to be the Bouillonville railway bridge. It spanned the valley and stream, Rupt de Mad. It was on the route from Nancy to Verdun. The village of Bouillonville is some 3km south-west of Thiaucourt. The bridge was either destroyed by the French in their retreat, or by the Germans early in the war. These photographs must have been taken before September 1918, as elements of the US 89th Division passed by the bridge on 12 September. They then moved into Bouillonville and captured a number of German prisoners. The woods that can be seen in the photograph were criss-crossed with barbed wire and filled with German machine guns. Much of the fighting was done in the woods. In the cemetery area near Bouillonville many German troops surrendered to the advancing Americans. The combat around this area was part of the Argonne offensive launched by both the French and the Americans.

This is a shot of what is believed to be one of the crossings on the Meuse River. This photograph would have been taken shortly before the US advance towards the river. Many of the smaller footbridges like this were destroyed, or badly damaged, which necessitated the US troops having to hastily throw up their own bridges to continue the offensive. In fact by the beginning of November 1918, US troops were advancing between the Meuse River and the Bois de Bourgogne, and making for Sedan. The US 3rd Corps swung to the east, led by the 5th Division. They crossed the Meuse and drove the Germans from Dun-sur-Meuse. On 9 November, continuing to exploit the river crossing, the US 3rd Corps continued pressing, by which time the US 1st and 5th Corps had also reached the Meuse River. At this stage the US troops had advanced over 40km since launching this new phase of the offensive on 1 November.

Here we can see the shattered remains of a French village in the Meuse region. The successful crossing of the Meuse was one of the key tipping points that finally convinced the Germans to sue for peace. There were already US plans to proceed with the offensive, and in fact between 7–10 November the US 3rd Corps pushed eastward toward Remoiville. Other US units, together with the 17th French Corps, pushed the Germans off the remaining heights to the east of the Meuse. The US 1st and 2nd Armies were urged to continue to push east. By the morning of 11 November the Meuse River line was firmly in Allied hands. But this would be the last phase of the operation, as the armistice had been signed and hostilities would soon cease.

This is a partially destroyed French church. Note the way in which the church has been constructed. It shows signs of its age by revealing the small, stone wall construction, which has been hidden by a later facade. It appears that the church tower itself has been targeted. These were popular posts for artillery observers, but they would also be the first targets to be pinpointed by the enemy in order to deny the artillery a view of the battlefield. Also note that the village shows signs that it has been prepared for defence, with coiled rows of barbed wire along the roadside and a chevaux-de-frise, constructed to pull across the road. This was an ancient, probably medieval invention, which had originally been a log with iron or wooden spikes hammered through it, and used as an anti-cavalry obstacle.

These are the remains of a concrete bunker that has received a direct hit and has been partially buried. Bunkers and pillboxes were developed during the First World War as a means to ensure defence in depth. Arguably they were probably first used in significant numbers on the Hindenburg Line. This was constructed during the winter of 1916–17 and it stretched from Lens to beyond Verdun. In effect, it was built across a salient, with the idea that German troops could fall back to these fortifications, thereby shortening their front. The withdrawal toward the Hindenburg Line began in February 1917. As the Germans withdrew and the Allies advanced, they moved into a devastated landscape.

This is one of the many ruined French towns close to the Hindenburg Line. The Germans fortified many of the villages, calling them outpost villages. These were reinforced, and were integral parts of the defensive lines. The idea was to use these outpost villages to slow the enemy down and disrupt their advance. It did, however, mean that the villages came under significant artillery fire from the Allies, and they were also badly damaged as a result of tenacious fighting, before the Germans would withdraw to their main defensive lines.

This appears to be ruins in Vigneulles-les-Hattonchatel, which was inside the St Mihiel salient. The Americans launched their offensive against the St Mihiel salient following their successful attack in the Aisne and Marne areas in August 1918. Some nine US divisions, amounting to 550,000 troops and supported by 70,000 French in four more divisions, were mobilized against the salient's defenders, which were reckoned to be around 60,000 Germans. The US 1st Army progressed five miles on 12 September, moving in on Vigneulles-les-Hattonchatel from the south and the west. Some 16,000 Germans were trapped and forced to surrender by the following day. Three days later, at a cost of 7,000 US casualties, the salient had been eliminated.

This photograph features a heavily destroyed French building that is showing signs of defensive positions. The Hindenburg Line aimed to straighten out the main German defensive line. The idea was to reduce the frontage of the German line by as much as 50km. In doing so, ten divisions of infantry and over fifty batteries of artillery would be released from immediate front-line duties and could then be used as a reserve. The area that was sacrificed in order to do this was flattened and mines were laid. The Germans built the 160km line between Lens and Reims in five months using 500,000 labourers. It was a huge network of trenches and dugouts, all protected by a barbed wire belt of 20 metres. Some of these defensive lines were made of reinforced concrete. About 1km in front of the main defensive lines was the outpost line and then another zone that had been zeroed in by artillery.

This is a destroyed French village. This photograph was taken in the winter months of 1918. As the war in Europe moved towards a close in November 1918 the last two months of the war brought in wintry winds and rain. There was even sleet and snow, as well as fog. Back on 8 August 1918, after the decisive victory at Amiens, the Allies launched their so-called 100 Days Offensive. In September, Allied forces bombarded the Hindenburg Line, and in the last twenty-four hours the British artillery alone, fired 945,000 shells at the German defensive lines. They captured the St Quentin Canal, and to do this they used a creeping barrage, and the line was successfully breached by 9 September.

This photograph shows relative calm in a heavily damaged French village. The last major Allied offensive had a high degree of poignancy. In the northern part of the operations British and Belgian troops launched their assault on 28 September 1918. They crossed the old Ypres battlefield and within three days had taken the men in Road Ridge, Passchendaele Ridge, and many other landmarks that had seen ruinous fighting for four years. Essentially, this phase of the operation was to become known as the fourth battle of Ypres. Mud and rain now delayed them and the new offensive reopened on 14 October. The British and Belgian troops were facing one of the tougher parts of the German line, and in fact they were still outnumbered by the Germans. Some forty British divisions, supported by US troops, were facing fifty-seven German divisions who had had the advantage of being able to dig in and construct formidable fortifications.

Another photograph of the same French village, as German soldiers emerge from their cellar shelters.

Chapter Seven

Official Photographs

The majority of images of the First World War are in black and white, or rather in shades of grey. These seem to match the terrible events of that war. Even this small collection, gleaned from the archives of the US Library of Congress, is in sharp, black and white detail. Yet we have to remember that in many respects the First World War was not just a black and white conflict. Even in the hell of the trench warfare there was colour, perhaps the most vibrant of which was the blood red poppies.

It was not until relatively recently that the existence of colour photographs became known. The Germans had some nineteen official war photographers, who were charged with chronicling the events of the war. One of these men, who would later go on to provide photographs for the *National Geographic* magazine, was Hans Hildenbrand. He actually shot his photographs in colour.

Hans Hildenbrand was born in 1870 and was a Stuttgart-based photographer and had been experimenting with auto chromes since 1909. Essentially this was three-colour photography, using the principle that all colours were a combination of the colours red, green and blue. The idea had been developed almost certainly in France. There were also other photographers using this new experimental form of photography, including British, Australian and French. It is believed that colour photography had existed since 1879, but even during the First World War it was relatively uncommon.

This small collection of photographs is uncredited and has probably been gleaned from a number of individual prints, albums, collections or archives over the decades since the First World War. The photographs that we have seen elsewhere in the book were almost certainly taken by a gifted German amateur, or perhaps an individual, possibly an officer, with sufficient photographic knowledge and the ability to have his photographs processed. This would have been a rare opportunity, and may infer that the photographer had access to a rear area where he could set up a dark room to process his prints.

It is likely that these Library of Congress photographs are in fact official. Unlike many photographs of this period none of them appear to have been retouched. Retouching was a common technique, and in some cases it would have been used to obliterate any geographical references, primarily for security reasons. Sometimes faces would also be partially obscured and the more savage realities of war would be censored out.

It is certainly the case that photography was a popular pastime. It is believed that tens of thousands of German soldiers took their cameras with them to war. Many of these amateur photographs lay undiscovered for years, but they do provide a very authentic view of the German perspective of the Western Front. It is interesting to note that undoubtedly some of the photographs in this Library of Congress collection are almost certainly posed, notably the trench scenes. This is in stark contrast to the more amateur nature of many of the other photographs in this book, which are more spontaneous. They give an entirely different view of the war compared to those taken by official photographers, whose responsibility it would be to take professional photographs for newspapers, or indeed chronicled events for propaganda purposes.

The gradual rediscovery of German photographs, particularly the amateur ones of the First World War, gives us an entirely new perspective on the conflict.

This photograph shows a lull in the fighting. The German soldiers are enjoying a rest, catching up on their reading and scanning their letters from home. Note the individual at the front of the trench line, to the rear of the photograph. He has taken up a firing position and is clearly on sentry duty. Also note the grooves in the front of the trench line. These have been designed so that the rifles fit into the slots and give the soldiers a few more inches of cover from enemy fire. *(Library of Congress)*

Here we can see a Renault FT light tank. It had a rotating turret and was armed with a 37mm gun. The FT was the first operational tank with a rotating turret. The French had all sorts of problems with the prototypes and, as a result, only eighty-four had been produced by the end of 1917. Nonetheless, 2,697 were produced by the end of the war. The FT would be widely used by both the French and the United States. It was extremely cheap and very easy to produce in mass. The intention was to produce more than 12,000 of them before the end of 1919. It would become an incredibly successful tank, being exported to a host of different countries. Incredibly, it was still in service, albeit obsolete, for the Second World War. The Germans, after the fall of France, captured more than 1,700 of them and they used them for patrolling occupied Europe, and for defending airfields. They were also used by the Germans in their attempts to stem the tide against the French resistance in Paris in 1944.

This photograph was taken at Saint Michel in France, and its original caption suggests that it is leaving the Allied lines, *en route* towards the German trench lines. If the caption is correct then this tank is in fact an American one. On 12–14 September 1918 the Americans, led by General John J. Pershing, were involved in the launching of a major offensive against a German salient, which had been in existence since 1914. The battle took place on the Mers River, to the east of Paris. The offensive (also known as Saint Mihiel) caught the Germans unprepared, as they were already falling back. *(Library of Congress)*

This photograph shows a German sniper. It depicts a man who is clearly exhausted. He is armed with a standard 7.92mm Mauser *Gewehr* 98, which was designed by Peter Paul Mauser in 1898. It was a robust design, which incorporated the clip and magazine in a single, detachable mechanism. This meant that it was easier to reload. It was not, however, a great weapon for rapid-fire, as it used a bolt mechanism and the magazine only carried five rounds. This was a very dependable weapon, and although this particular one does not have an optical sight, it was often used as a sniper's weapon. The British would have used a Lee Enfield short magazine Mark III, with a ten cartridge magazine. The French would have used a Lebel 8mm 1866 model, or a Berthier with a three-round magazine (later five-round). The Americans used a Springfield and the Austro-Hungarians a Repetier *Gewehr* M95. (*Library of Congress*)

A photograph showing a German horse-drawn artillery gun being wheeled into position can be seen here. Horse-drawn artillery was extensively used during the First World War. In fact, with some minor alteration to the uniform, this would have been a typical sight during the Second World War too. Many of the German artillery units were still horse-drawn until as late as 1945. This particular artillery piece is almost certainly a 77mm weapon that was developed by Krupp and produced between 1916 and 1918. (*Library of Congress*)

This photograph is captioned as 'German troops marching towards Albert in France'. The town of Albert is located between Amiens and Bapaume in the Somme Department of Picardie in northern France. It is particularly well known as the site of the battle of the Somme, which took place between 1 July and 18 November 1916. Although it is unclear from this photograph, this shot may well have been taken in March 1918 when the Germans recaptured the town during their spring offensive. The British held the town at the time, and bombarded the basilica of Notre Dame de Brebières to destroy the church tower in an attempt to prevent the Germans from using it as an observation position. The Germans were forced to retreat from Albert in August 1918, at which point the British reoccupied the town. (*Library of Congress*)

This is a posed photograph of what appears to be unarmed German troops amidst a devastated landscape. It features the remnants of a trench system, with dugout shelters. Note the wooden duckboards in the bottom of the trench as a partial attempt to prevent the soldiers from sinking into the mud. Clearly visible are manmade structures, some of which are now only partially buried. Some trench systems were under constant bombardment for months on end; other trench networks regularly changed hands, requiring additional work and repair. Note also the complete absence of vegetation. In no part of this photograph are there any signs of trees or bushes. This is clearly an area of the front that has been fought over for a considerable number of months. In all likelihood this photograph was taken towards the end of the First World War. (*Library of Congress*)

Here we have a fascinating photograph, as it clearly depicts a British tank that has been captured and pressed into service by the Germans. We know of several instances of British tanks having been captured, for example, tank number 799 was captured near Arras on 11 April 1917. There were certainly a considerable number of Allied tanks that fell into German hands. Many early attempts to use the tanks in difficult terrain led to breakdowns, which, in the heat of battle meant that the vehicle had to be abandoned. The British first deployed their Mark I tanks in the battle of the Somme on 15 September 1916. Of the forty-nine shipped to the battlefield, thirty-two were serviceable and took part in the attack; only nine made it to the German lines. The first really successful use of tanks took place at Cambrai in 1917. When the Germans deployed their tank force at the second battle of Villers-Bretonneux, between 24–27 April 1918, the majority of the 100 or so tanks that they fielded were actually captured British or French models. On 24 April the first tank versus tank engagement took place, when three German A7Vs engaged three British Mark IVs. (*Library of Congress*)

This is a German convoy that is proceeding along the road. Note that the vast majority are horse-drawn transports. On the Western Front alone, at least 8 million horses were killed during the course of the First World War. The Germans had actually set up their own breeding programme for horses and mules. The idea was to increase the ratio of horses to men from around 1:4 in the late nineteenth century, to 1:3 by 1914. The Germans alone mobilised over 700,000 horses in the first few weeks of the war. The casualty rate for horses was at least 25 per cent. The horse had, of course, been used in the early weeks of the war in its conventional role as a cavalry mount. This was before the war resulted in trench warfare stalemate along the majority of the front. Horses were still used by cavalry in the Middle East, notably in Palestine. (*Library of Congress*)

German infantry are in a zigzag trench line in this photograph. Note the town that is just visible in the background. It is not possible to identify the location of this photograph, but it is typical of trench lines that were built either at the extreme of an advance, or as a fall-back position beyond the main trench lines. Given time, the trench system would become more sophisticated, and there would be trench lines stretching back into rear areas, in order to provide cover for resupply, and there would be more permanent and secure (relatively) bunkers. These bunkers would enable the soldier to shelter from artillery bombardments. The idea of the trench was to defend your own position whilst trying to break through into the rear of the enemy trench lines. In effect it was a war of attrition. This had not been the nature of warfare in the early weeks of the First World War, but after the breaking of the main German defence lines towards the end of the war, a more fluid system was once again adopted. (*Library of Congress*)

GERMANS IN THE "ARGONNE"

This photograph is captioned 'Germans in the Argonne'. Although undated, one of the major actions that took place in this part of the battlefield occurred between 26 September and 11 November 1918. It was known as the so-called 'Triple Offensive'. Essentially it was a Franco-American assault and it began on 26 September. Over the next five days the Allies advanced deep into German lines. Part of the fight took place in the Argonne Forest, which is the probable location of this building. In all likelihood this photograph was taken considerably before the offensive of 1918. The Meuse-Argonne Offensive was of particular importance to the Americans, as it was arguably the largest battle that had been fought by the American Expeditionary Force. The battle was to cost the Americans 117,000 casualties, the French lost 70,000 and the Germans at least 100,000. The offensive is particularly noteworthy, as the casualties represent a staggering 40 per cent of all US losses throughout the course of their involvement in the war. (*Library of Congress*)

GERMAN SNIPER

20

Another picture of a German sniper can be seen here; this time the sniper lies prone behind a barbed wire entanglement. He is wearing a *Pickelhaube*, or spiked helmet. This suggests that the photograph was taken fairly early on in the First World War. A simplified model of the helmet was introduced, which had a detachable spike. In fact, by September 1915, German soldiers were ordered to remove the spike from their helmets whilst in the front line. The vast majority of them were made from leather, which offered virtually no protection from shrapnel. It was also obvious that the spike provided a good aiming point for enemy snipers. By the beginning of 1916 the *Pickelhaube* was replaced by a steel helmet. This reduced head shot fatalities by at least 70 per cent. The *Pickelhaube* was reduced to ceremonial duties only, usually only being worn by senior officers. (*Library of Congress*)

A wrecked German truck is featured here. It appears from the photograph that this vehicle once housed an artillery piece, as it has clearly visible stabilisers, which would have been used to provide a more solid gun platform. This may well be a German 77mm anti-aircraft gun. They were often truck mounted and used as anti-tank weapons. Alternatively, it could be a British truck mounted 3-inch anti-aircraft gun that has been mounted on a Peerless lorry, which was remarkably similar. *(Library of Congress)*

This photograph shows a German trench system snaking away into the distance in a levelled landscape. The primary focus is on a German machine-gun team. The machine gun appears to be a standard *Maschinengewehr* 08. As its name suggests it was adopted in 1908, but was based on an earlier 1901 model, which in turn was almost a copy of Hiram Maxim's 1884 model. The weapon was water-cooled, and could fire 7.92mm rounds at a rate of up to 400 per minute from a 250-round fabric belt. It had a range of up to 4,000m and the German army embraced this weapon wholeheartedly. By 1916 they were producing over 14,000 of them per month. New versions came into production over the course of the war, including the MG08/15, which had a bipod and the MG08/18, which was air-cooled. This later model was primarily designed for offensive warfare rather than simply a defensive weapon. (*Library of Congress*)

Another shot can be seen here of German troops in a trench system. Note the wickerwork fencing, designed to hold back the rear bank of the trench. There is also wickerwork used in front of the forward firing step, again to provide some solidity to the trench system. This trench appears to have been built on relatively high ground. This would afford the Germans considerable advantage in terms of observation. Note also the protective metal shields, which have been set-up along the front of the trench line. They incorporate slots through which a rifle can be poked, but afford the rifleman protection from incoming enemy shots. It is likely that this photograph was taken early on in the war, as the rifleman in the foreground is wearing a *Pickelhaube*. (*Library of Congress*)

7981

This photograph is captioned as depicting an abandoned British trench system and featuring German cavalry. The Germans, as did the Allies during the war, deployed large numbers of cavalry units. There was still a wide range of different types of cavalry, and it appears from this photograph that at least some of the men are armed with lances. Both Britain and Germany, when war broke out, had cavalry forces that numbered at least 100,000 men each. However, as far as the Western Front was concerned, the last cavalry charge was probably at Mons. There is a reference to a cavalry charge in the spring of 1918, when British cavalry charged German infantry; they were cut to pieces by German machine guns.

At the outbreak of the war the German cavalry was considered to be the elite, and may have totalled as many as 550 squadrons. They were originally earmarked to provide protection to the flanks of the main German attack in 1914, but it soon became abundantly clear that they could play little role in the static trench warfare that later developed. (*Library of Congress*)

This is a photograph of a wrecked German Albatross. The Albatross was a biplane. The prototypes had been tested in 1916 and an initial order for fifty aircraft was placed in early 1917. The first operational aircraft actually entered service in December 1916. In all, just less than 1,900 were built. It had a top speed of around 170km/h, a range of 480km, and had a pair of 7.92mm machine guns. Several famous German aces flew this aircraft, the Albatross DIII, including Manfred von Richthofen, Karl Emil Schäfer and Kurt Wolff. The aircraft had its high point in the so-called 'Bloody April' of 1917, when the Albatross outperformed available British and French fighters, which led to the loss, for the British, of 245 aircraft, against sixty-six German losses. This was the last time that the Germans had air superiority. With the introduction of better aircraft, including the Sopwith Camel, the SE5 and the Spad SXIII, the battle for air supremacy was never really challenged again by the Germans. (*Library of Congress*)

This photograph is captioned 'Observation from German trenches'. It shows a pair of German officers gingerly squinting through the narrow eye slit in a metal plate, propped up on the front trench line. Note the depth of the trench and how it affords the Germans almost complete protection from direct fire from the enemy trench line. This is a solidly built trench system.

Bibliography

Banks, Arthur, *A Military Atlas of the First World War*, Pen & Sword Books, 2000.

Cross, Robin, *World War One in Photographs*, Parragon, 1996.

Gleichen, Edward, *Chronology of the Great War*, Pen & Sword Books, 2000.

Guest, Philip and Helen McPhail, *St Quentin*, Pen & Sword Books, 2000.

Keegan, John, *The First World War*, Vintage, 2000.

Lewinski, Jorge, *The Camera At War*, W.H. Allen, 1978.

Pit, Barrie, *1918: The Last Act*, Pen & Sword Books, 2003.

Simkins, Peter, *World War One*, Colour Library Books, 1992.

Stedman, Michael, *Advance to Victory 1918*, Pen & Sword Books, 1999.

Notes

Notes